Contents

Stream or download the video, audio & software content for this book. To access online content, visit:
www.alfred.com/redeem
Enter the following code: 00-44100_882288

Revised Edition
Copyright © 2012, 2014 by Alfred Music
All rights reserved. Printed in USA.

Alfred Music
P.O. Box 10003
Van Nuys, CA 91410-0003
alfred.com

ISBN-10: 1-4706-1986-5
ISBN-13: 978-1-4706-1986-2

Cover photograph: Courtesy of Gibson Musical Instruments.

Audio recorded Third Encore Studios, Burbank, CA; Sandy Brook Studios, Colebrook, CT. Mandolin and guitar recorded by Jared Meeker and Paul Howard.

The Parts of Your Mandolin

THE MANDOLIN

Tuning Pegs → Headstock ←

String Numbers → 4321 Nut ←

Strings/Courses —

Fingerboard —

Frets

Strap Button —

Neck ←

Pick Guard —

F-hole —

Body ←

Bridge

Tail Piece —

Strap Button →

In addition to the MP3 demonstrations and backing tracks, the online media includes Alfred's exclusive TNT 2 software, which allows users to customize the audio tracks in this book for practice. Use it to slow down tracks, isolate and loop parts, and change tempos and keys.

To download TNT 2, refer to the instructions on page 1.

TNT 2 SYSTEM REQUIREMENTS

Windows
10, 8, 7
QuickTime 7.6.7 or higher
1.8 GHz processor or faster
500 MB hard drive space
2 GB RAM minimum
Speakers or headphones
Internet access for updates

Macintosh
OS 10.4 and higher (Intel only)
QuickTime 7.6.7 or higher
600 MB hard drive space
2 GB RAM minimum
Speakers or headphones
Internet access for updates

How to Hold Your Mandolin

Standing

Cradle the mandolin with your right arm by gently holding it close to your body. If you have a strap, you can place it behind your neck or over just one shoulder. Your right hand should be relaxed and free to strum. Keep your left wrist away from the fingerboard to allow your fingers to be in a better position to finger the chords.

Sitting

Rest the mandolin gently on your right thigh and let your arms hang loosely and comfortably.

Courses and Strings

The strings on the mandolin are set up in four sets of two strings with each set tuned to the same note. Each pair of strings is called a *course*. The mandolin has four courses for a total of eight strings. In this book, we will always refer to each course as a string, so even though we say to play the "first string," we mean for you to play the "first set of strings."

Caring for Your Mandolin

A mandolin is a delicate wooden instrument, so make sure to treat it gently when you are playing or storing it. When you carry your mandolin, think of it as part of your body so you don't accidentally bump it against anything, and especially make sure not to drop it. Every time you are done playing, carefully dust off your mandolin with a soft cloth and put it away in its case.

The Right Hand

To strum means to play the strings with your right hand by brushing quickly across them with a *pick*. Picks come in a variety of shapes and sizes. Start off with a medium gauge pick.

Top

Actual size

Point

Strumming with a Pick

Hold the pick between your thumb and index finger. Hold it firmly, but don't squeeze it too hard.

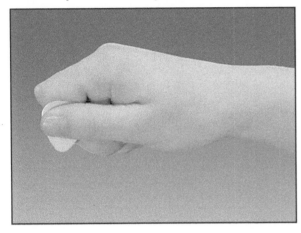

Strum from the fourth string (the course closest to the ceiling) to the first string (the course closest to the floor).

Important: Always strum by mainly moving your wrist, not just your arm. Use as little motion as possible. Start as close to the top string as you can, and never let your hand move past the edge of the mandolin.

Start just above the fourth string.

Move mostly your wrist, not just your arm. Finish just below the first string.

Picking Individual Strings

When picking single notes, start off just above the string and strum across just one course of strings. Stop the downward motion of the pick just after you pick the note. When picking on the second, third, and fourth strings, you need to stop the motion of the pick before you strike the next course of strings.

The Left Hand

Hand Position

Learning to use your left-hand fingers starts with good hand position. Place your hand so your thumb rests comfortably in the middle of the back of the neck of the mandolin. Position your fingers on the front of the neck as if you are gently squeezing a ball between them and your thumb. Keep your elbow in and your fingers curved.

Keep elbow in and fingers curved.

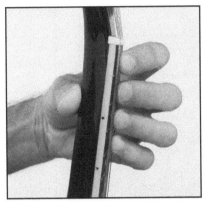

Like squeezing a small ball or making a small letter "c" with your fingers and thumb.

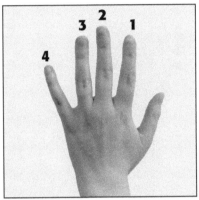

Left-hand fingers are numbered 1 through 4.

Placing a Finger on a String

When you press a string with a left-hand finger, make sure you press firmly with the tip of your finger and as close to the fret wire as you can without actually being right on it. Short fingernails are important! This will create a clean, bright tone.

RIGHT
Finger pressed the strings down near the fret without actually being on it.

WRONG
Finger is too far from fret wire; tone is "buzzy" and indefinite.

WRONG
Finger is on top of fret wire; tone is muffled and unclear.

How to Tune Your Mandolin

Tuning the strings of the mandolin can be tricky at first. You may want to have someone at your local music store help you out. Once you have done it a few times it will get easier, so be patient.

First, make sure your strings are wound properly around the tuning pegs. The four on the left should go from the inside to the outside, and the four on the right should go from the outside to the inside.

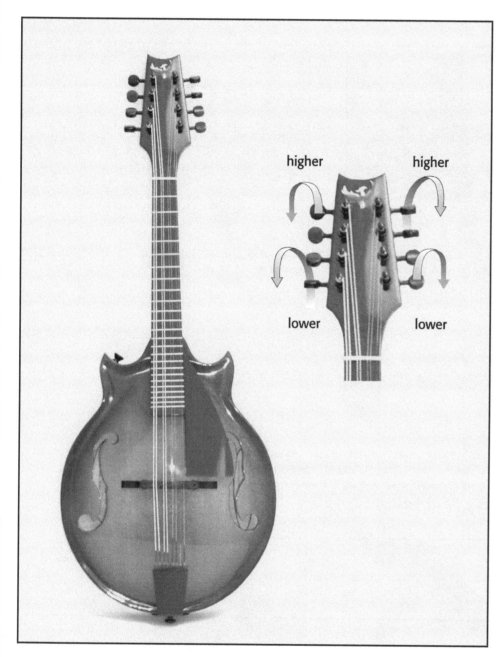

Be sure not to tune the strings too high because they could break!

Tuning with the Audio Track 1

Play track 1 of the recording. Listen to the pitches and match each of your mandolin's strings to the corresponding pitches. Since each course is made up of two strings that are tuned to the same pitch, you will have to tune one string at a time. First match the pitch of one of the strings and then match the other string to the pitch of the string you just tuned. Repeat this for each set of strings.

Tuning without the Audio

Tuning the Mandolin to Itself

When your fourth string is in tune, you can tune the rest of the strings just using the mandolin alone. First tune the fourth string to G on the piano, and then follow the instructions to get the mandolin in tune.

Press fret 7 of string 4 and tune the open string 3 to the pitch of string 4 (D).

Press fret 7 of string 3 and tune the open string 2 to the pitch of string 3 (A).

Press fret 7 of string 2 and tune the open string 1 to the pitch of string 2 (E).

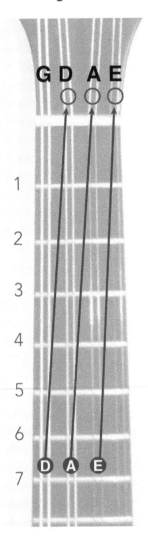

When tuning to a piano, match the fourth string to the G below Middle C.

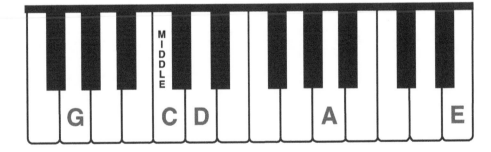

Pitch Pipes and Electronic Tuners

If you don't have a piano available, buying an electronic tuner, tuning app, or pitch pipe is recommended. The salesperson at your music store can show you how to use them.

Getting Acquainted with Music

Musical sounds are indicated by symbols called *notes*. Their time value is determined by their color (white or black) and by stems or flags attached to the note head.

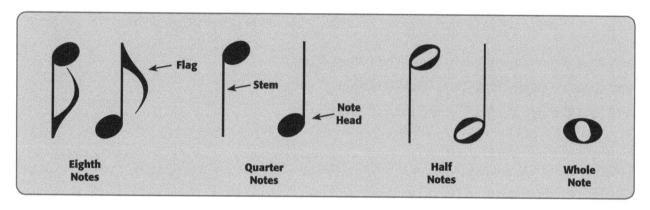

The Staff

The notes are named after the first seven letters of the alphabet (A–G), endlessly repeated to embrace the entire range of musical sound. The name and pitch of the note is determined by its position on five horizontal lines and the spaces between, called the *staff*.

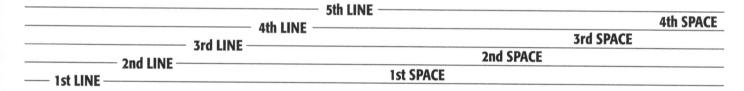

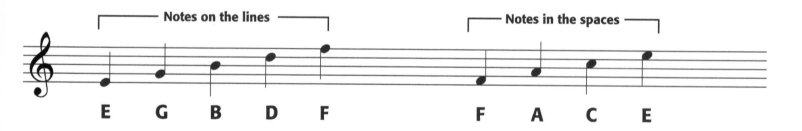

Measures

Music is divided into equal parts called *measures*, or *bars*. One measure is divided from another by a *bar line*.

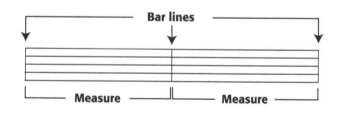

Clefs

During the evolution of musical notation, the staff had from 2 to 20 lines, and symbols were invented to locate certain lines and the pitch of the note on that line. These symbols are called *clefs*.

Music for mandolin is written in the *G clef*, or *treble clef*. Originally, the Gothic letter G was used on a four-line staff to establish the pitch of G.

This grew into the modern notation on a five-line staff:

Reading TAB

All the music in this book is written two ways: in standard music notation and TAB.

Below each standard music staff you'll find a four-line TAB staff. Each line in TAB represents a string of the mandolin, with the first string at the top and the fourth string at the bottom.

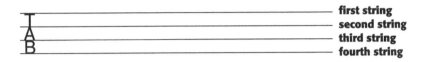

Numbers placed on the TAB lines tell you which fret to play. An "o" means to play the string open (not fingered).

| first string
3rd fret | second string
1st fret | third string
open | fourth string
open |

By glancing at the TAB, you can immediately tell where to play a note. Although you can't tell exactly what the rhythm is from the TAB, the horizontal spacing of the numbers gives you a strong hint about how long or short the notes are to be played.

Chord Diagrams

Chord diagrams are used to indicate fingerings for chords. The example here means to place your 1st finger on the 1st fret, first string, place your 2nd finger on the 2nd fret, second string, then strum all four strings. The "o" symbols on the third and fourth strings indicate to play them open (not fingered).

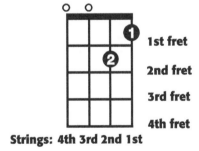

Strings: 4th 3rd 2nd 1st

The First String E

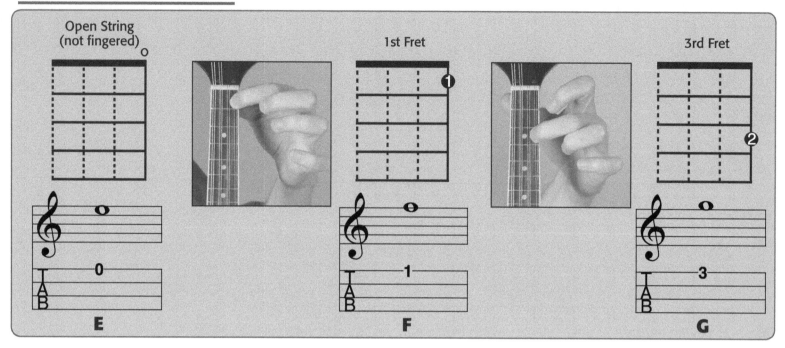

Play slowly and evenly. Use only downstrokes, indicated by ⊓. The symbol ○ over a note means *open string*. Do not finger.

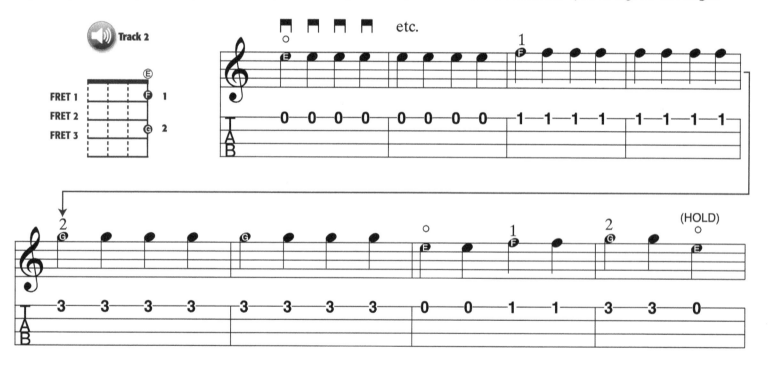

PLAYING WITH E, F, G Track 3

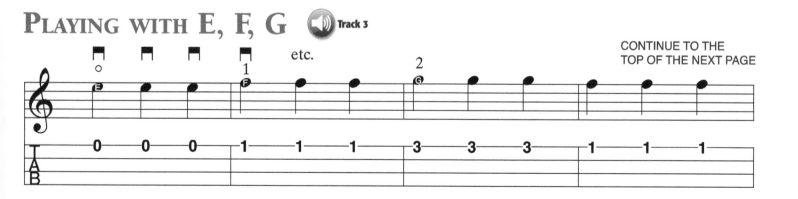

CONTINUE TO THE TOP OF THE NEXT PAGE

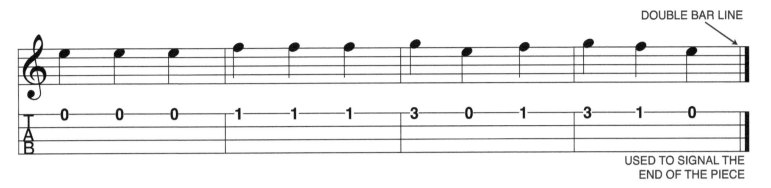

DOUBLE BAR LINE

USED TO SIGNAL THE
END OF THE PIECE

EXTRA CREDIT Track 4

Make sure to place your left-hand fingers as close to the fret wires as possible without touching them. When you play the F on the 1st fret and follow it with the G on the 3rd fret, keep the first finger down. You will only hear the G, but when you go back to the F, it will sound smooth.

Sound Off: How to Count Time

Four Kinds of Notes

Time Signatures

Each piece of music has numbers at the beginning called a *time signature*. These numbers tell us how to count time. The TOP NUMBER tells us how many counts are in each measure. The BOTTOM NUMBER tells us what kind of note gets one count.

FOUR COUNTS TO A MEASURE

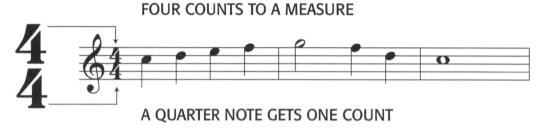

A QUARTER NOTE GETS ONE COUNT

THREE COUNTS TO A MEASURE

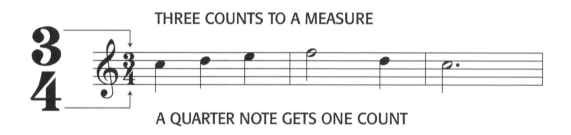

A QUARTER NOTE GETS ONE COUNT

TWO COUNTS TO A MEASURE

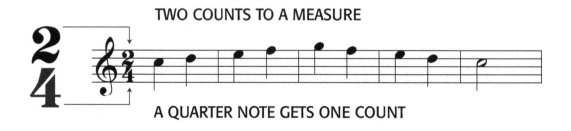

A QUARTER NOTE GETS ONE COUNT

Important: Go back and fill in the missing time signatures of the songs already learned.

Repeat Signs

This music uses *repeat signs.* The double dots inside the double bars tell you that everything between those double bars is to be repeated.

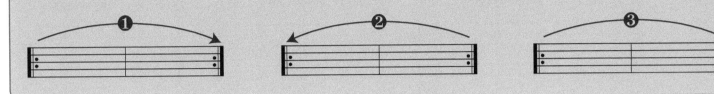

BLUES IN C   Track 5

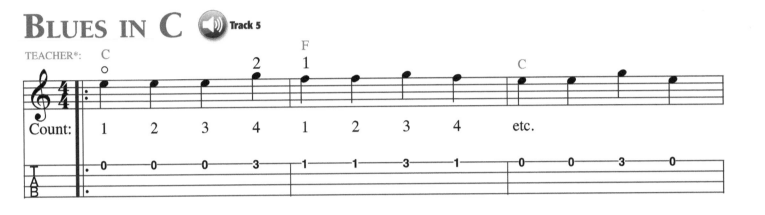

* Chords for your teacher to play, or that are played on the audio track and video.

The Second String A

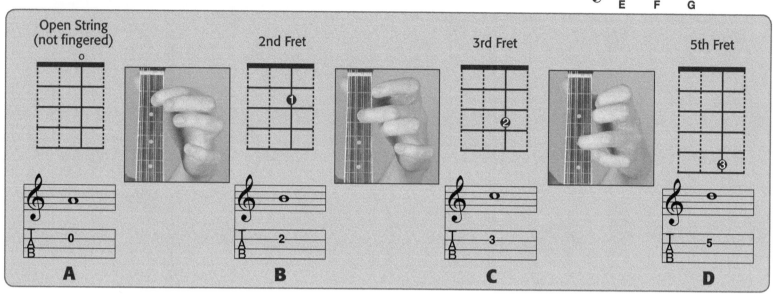

Open String (not fingered) — A

2nd Fret — B

3rd Fret — C

5th Fret — D

Track 6

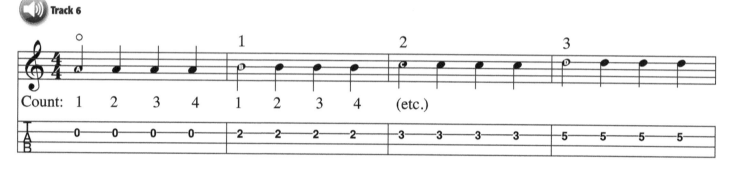

Count: 1 2 3 4 1 2 3 4 (etc.)

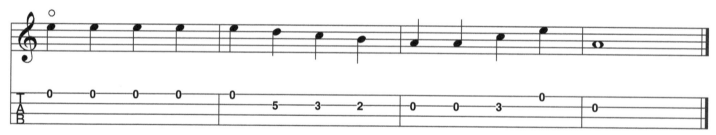

JAMMIN' ON TWO STRINGS   Track 7

TEACHER: C

Count: 1 2 3 4 (etc.)

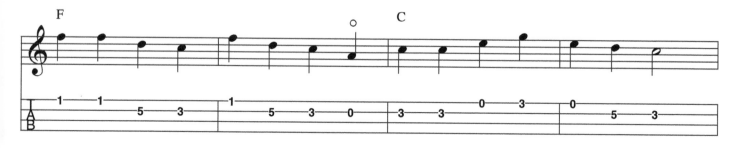

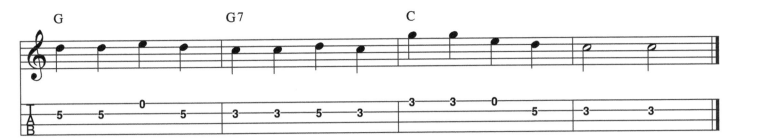

Hot Cross Buns

Track 8

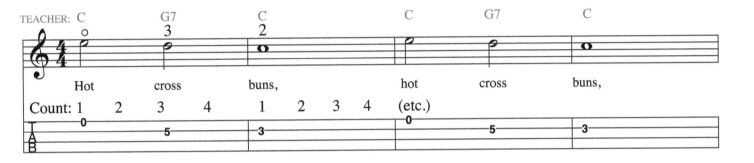

TEACHER:

Hot cross buns, hot cross buns,

Count: 1 2 3 4 1 2 3 4 (etc.)

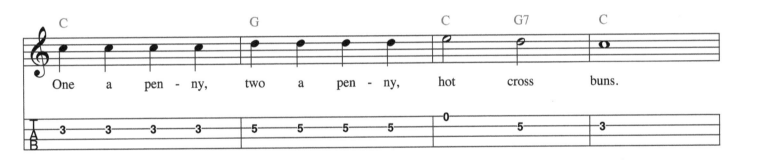

One a pen - ny, two a pen - ny, hot cross buns.

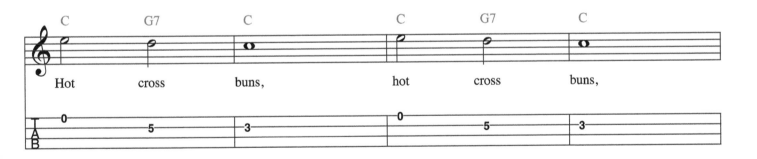

Hot cross buns, hot cross buns,

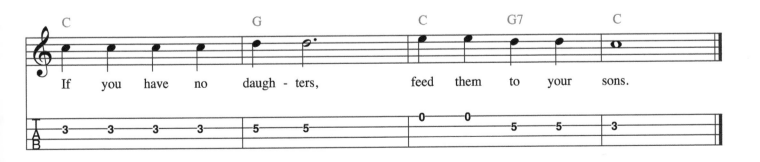

If you have no daugh - ters, feed them to your sons.

BLUES IN F   Track 9

TEACHER: F

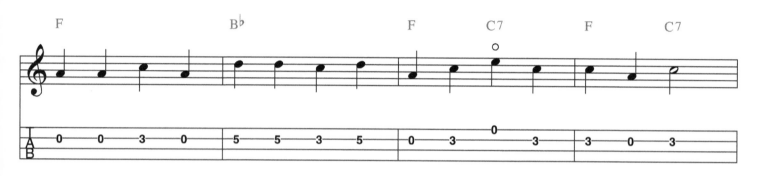

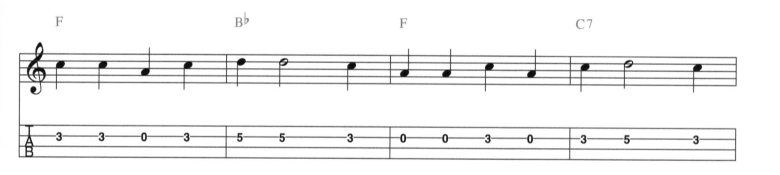

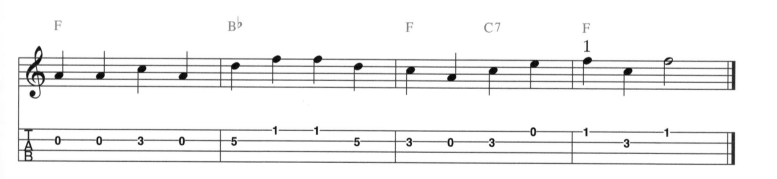

ROCKIN' MANDOLIN

Track 10

TEACHER:

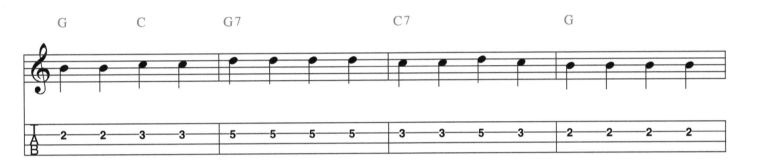

The Third String D

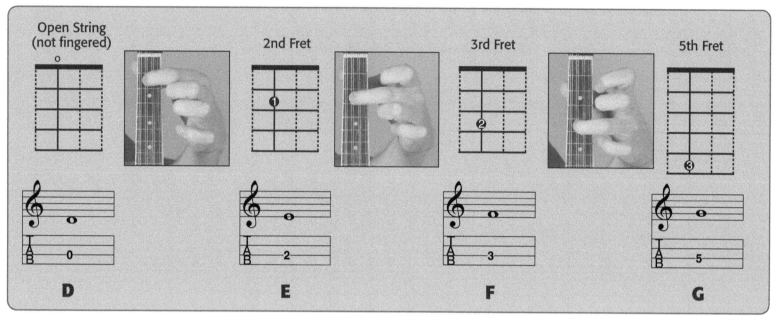

Open String (not fingered) — **D**

2nd Fret — **E**

3rd Fret — **F**

5th Fret — **G**

Track 11

OLD MacDonald Had a Farm Track 12

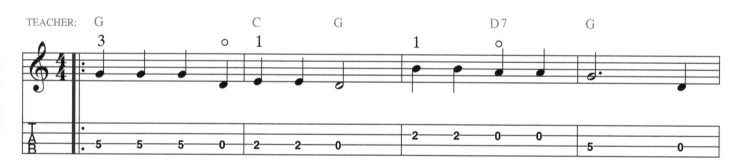

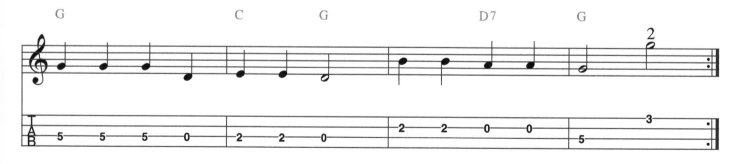

LARGO Track 13

(from *The New World Symphony*)

Antonin Dvořák

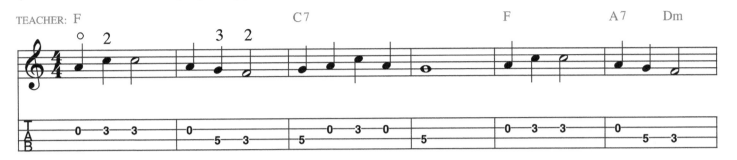

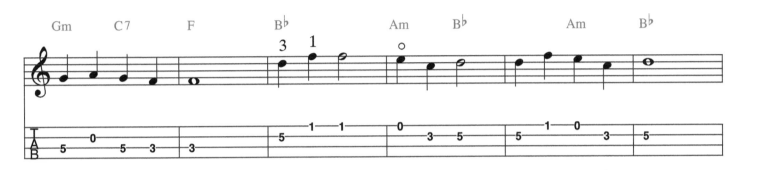

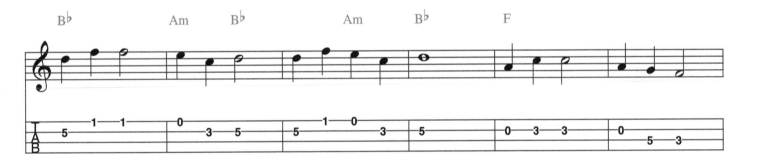

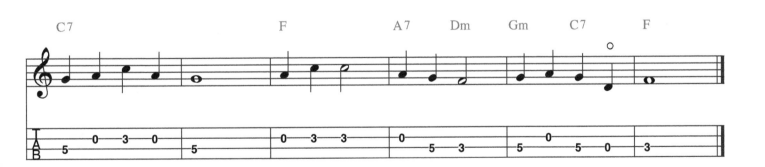

JINGLE BELLS

 Track 14

TEACHER: C

Jin - gle bells! Jin - gle bells! Jin - gle all the way! _____

F   C   D7   G7

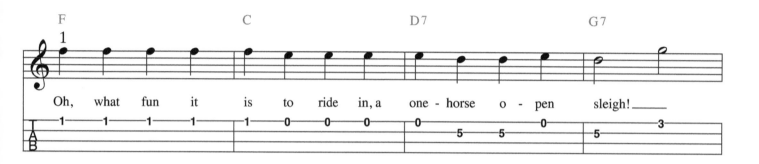

Oh, what fun it is to ride in, a one - horse o - pen sleigh! _____

C

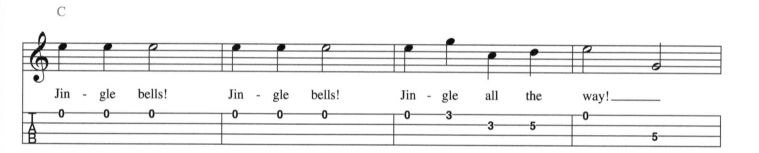

Jin - gle bells! Jin - gle bells! Jin - gle all the way! _____

F   C   G7   C

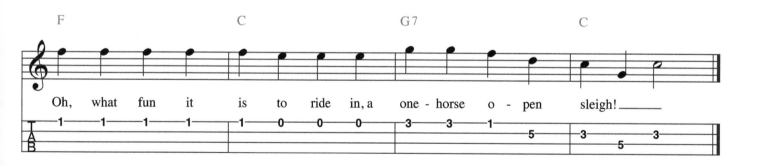

Oh, what fun it is to ride in, a one - horse o - pen sleigh! _____

BEAUTIFUL BROWN EYES Track 15

TEACHER: G

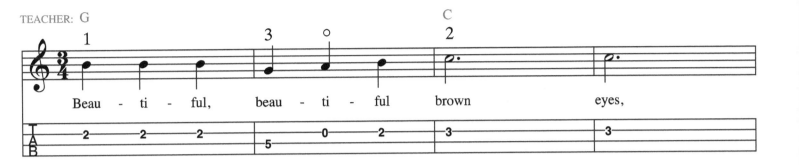

Beau - ti - ful, beau - ti - ful brown eyes,

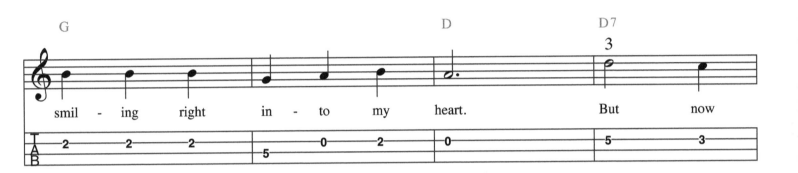

smil - ing right in - to my heart. But now

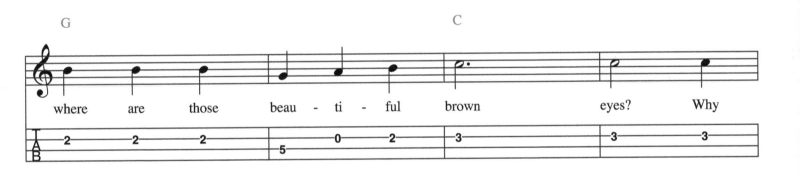

where are those beau - ti - ful brown eyes? Why

must we be so far a - part?_____

Introducing High A

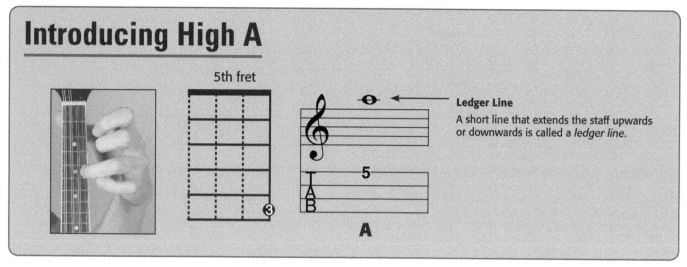

Ledger Line
A short line that extends the staff upwards or downwards is called a *ledger line.*

HIGH A EXERCISE   Track 16

ROCKIN' IN DORIAN MODE   Track 17

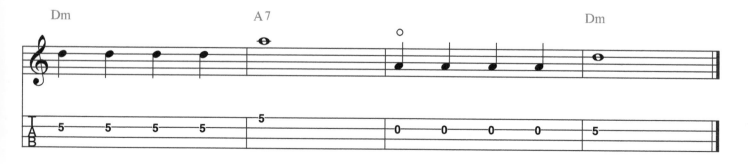

This traditional Scottish folk song became popular in the late 1870s and has been performed widely ever since. The Beatles even recorded a rock version of it with English singer Tony Sheridan in 1961.

MY BONNIE LIES OVER THE OCEAN Track 18

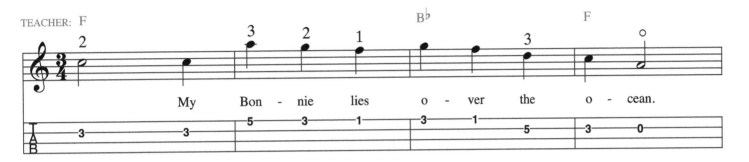

My Bon - nie lies o - ver the o - cean.

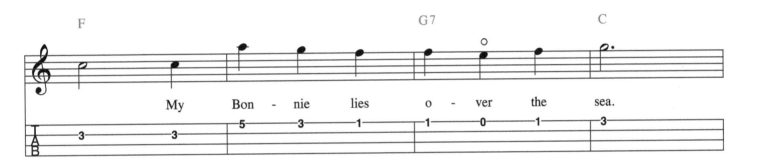

My Bon - nie lies o - ver the sea.

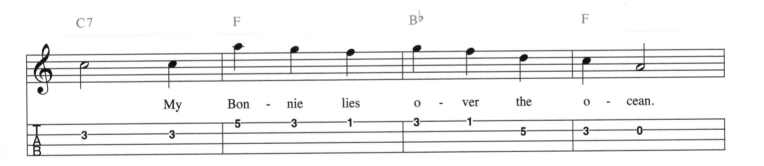

My Bon - nie lies o - ver the o - cean.

Oh bring back my Bon - nie to me.

24

The Fourth String G

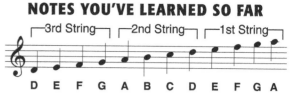

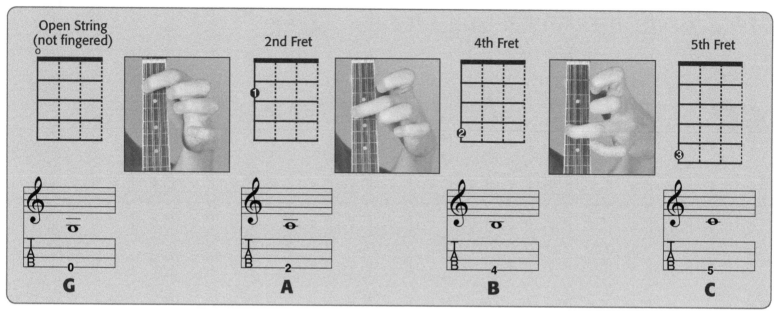

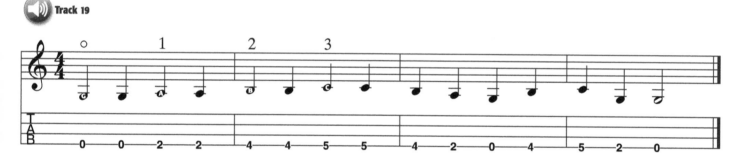

DRINK TO ME ONLY WITH THINE EYES

Track 20

Traditional

FOUR-STRING ROCK Track 21

TEACHER:

"Aura Lee" is an old American folk song that was later recorded by Elvis Presley as "Love Me Tender."

AURA LEE  Track 22

Traditional

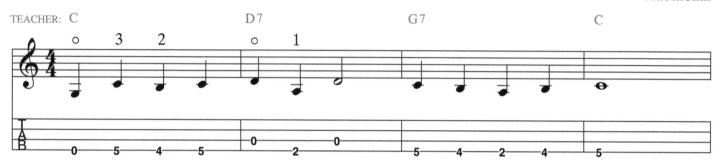

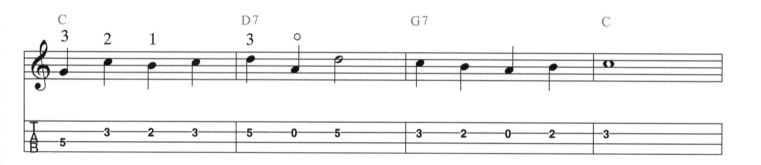

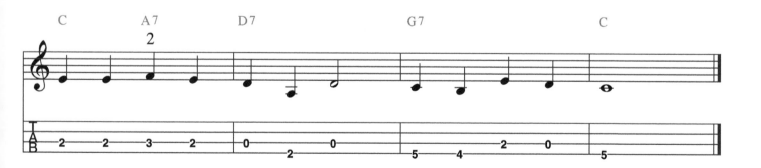

Au clair de la lune Track 23

French Folk Song

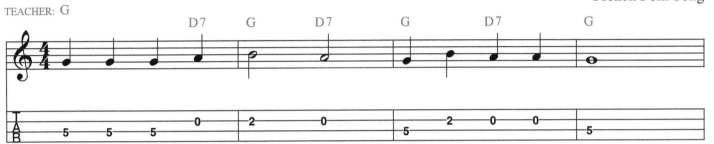

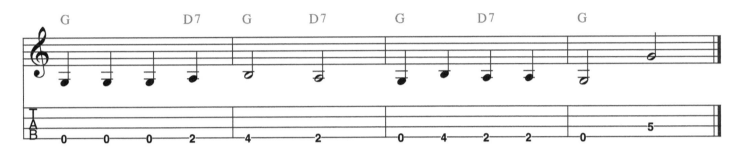

The Wearing o' the Green Track 24

Irish Ballad

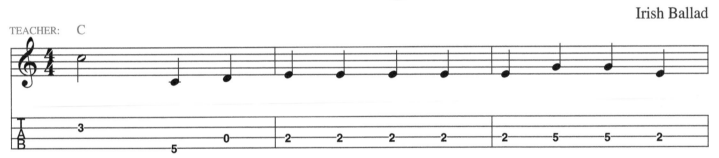

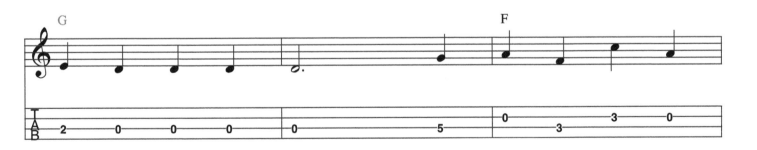

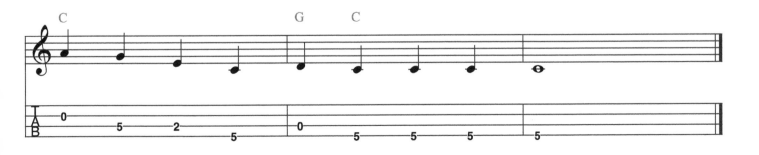

Tempo Signs

A *tempo sign* tells you how fast to play the music. Below are the three most common tempo signs, which are Italian words. In some music, you will see tempo signs written in English.

Andante ("ahn-DAHN-teh") means to play slow.

Moderato ("moh-deh-RAH-toh") means to play moderately.

Allegro ("ah-LAY-groh") means to play fast.

Quarter Rest

 This sign indicates silence for one count. For a clearer effect, you may stop the sound of the strings by touching the strings lightly with the heel of the right hand.

THREE-TEMPO ROCKIN' MANDOLIN

 Track 25 Track 26 Track 27

Play three times: first time Andante, second time Moderato, and third time Allegro.

Introducing Chords

A *chord* is a combination of harmonious notes.
All notes except the whole note have a stem going up or down.
When notes are struck together as a chord, they are connected by the same stem.

(Not to be played.)

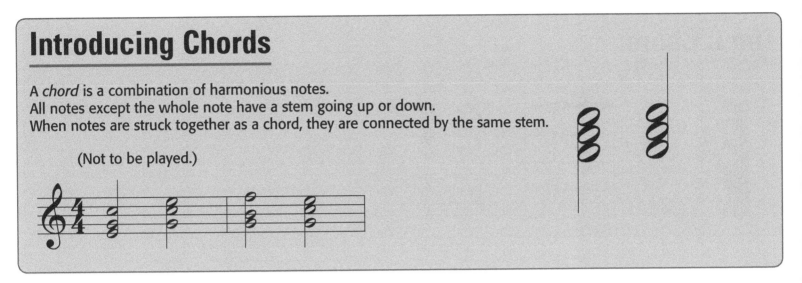

Let's get used to reading more than one note at a time and start by playing two open strings.

TWO-NOTE EXERCISE Track 28

In this example, you play three open strings.

THREE-NOTE EXERCISE  Track 29

In the four-note exercise, strum all four strings. Remember to start the strum just above the fourth string. Use mostly your wrist, and finish just below the 1st string.

FOUR-NOTE EXERCISE Track 30

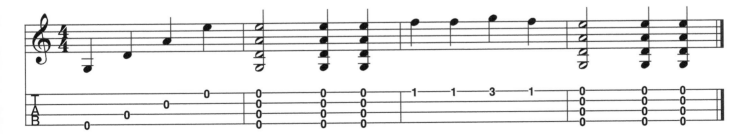

The C Chord

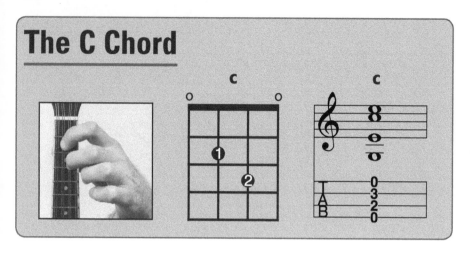

Track 31

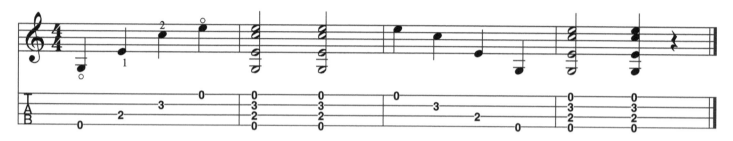

ODE TO JOY  Track 32

Ludwig van Beethoven

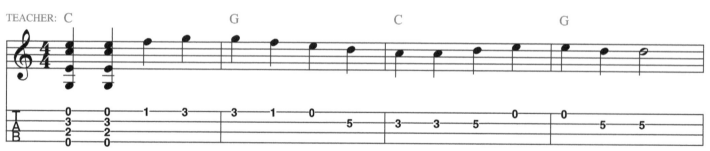

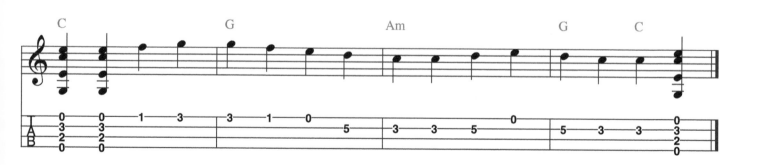

THE RIDDLE SONG Track 33

Traditional British

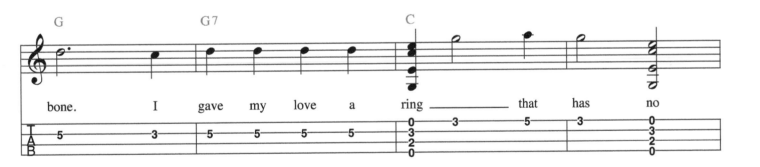

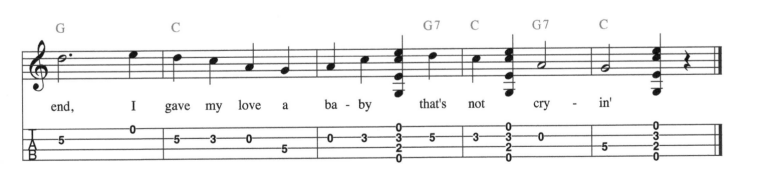

The G7 Chord

Another chord used below is:

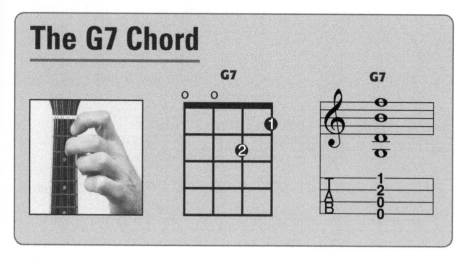

Two-Chord Waltz

Track 35

TEACHER: C

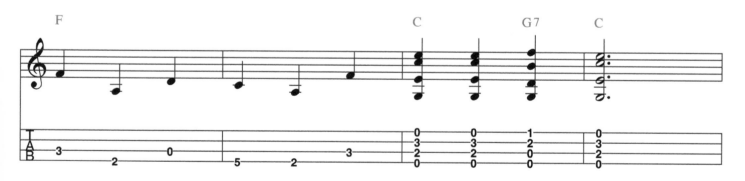

Here is a song for you to sing while you play the accompaniment. The slanting line following a chord symbol (C ✦✦✦ G7 ✦✦✦) means to play the same chord again for each line. Repeat the chord until a new chord symbol appears.

LOVE SOMEBODY

Track 36
Melody and Chords

Track 37
Chords Only

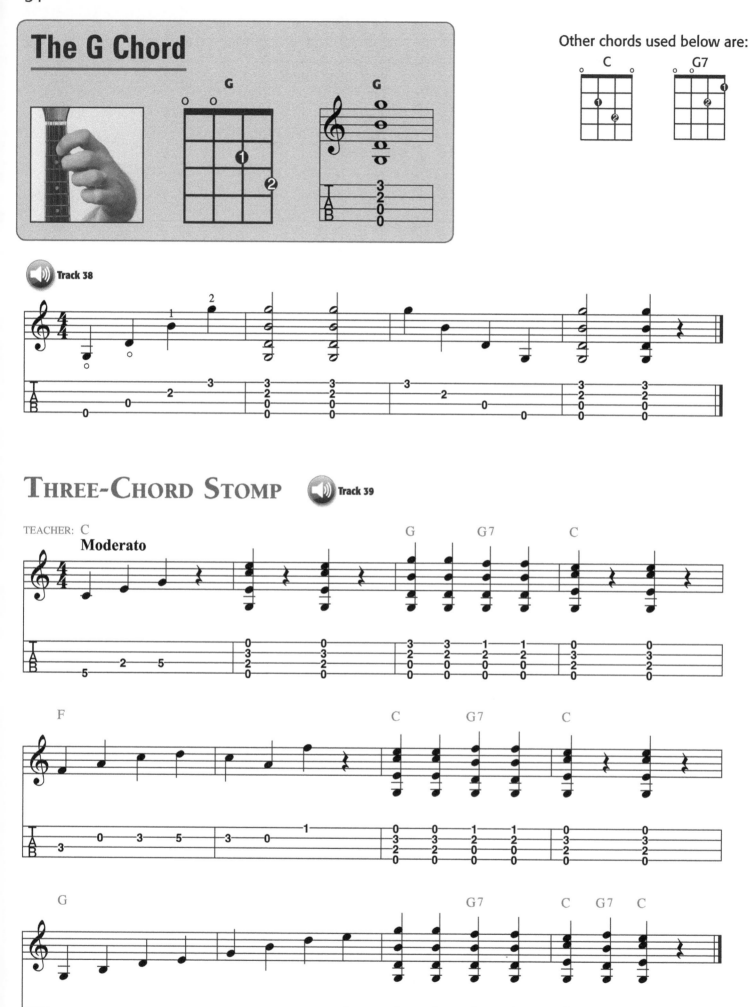

The G Chord

Other chords used below are:

Track 38

THREE-CHORD STOMP Track 39

TEACHER: C

Moderato

Incomplete Measures

Not all pieces of music begin on the first beat. Sometimes, music begins with an incomplete measure called a *pickup*. If the pickup is one beat, often the last measure will only have three beats in $\frac{4}{4}$, or two beats in $\frac{3}{4}$.

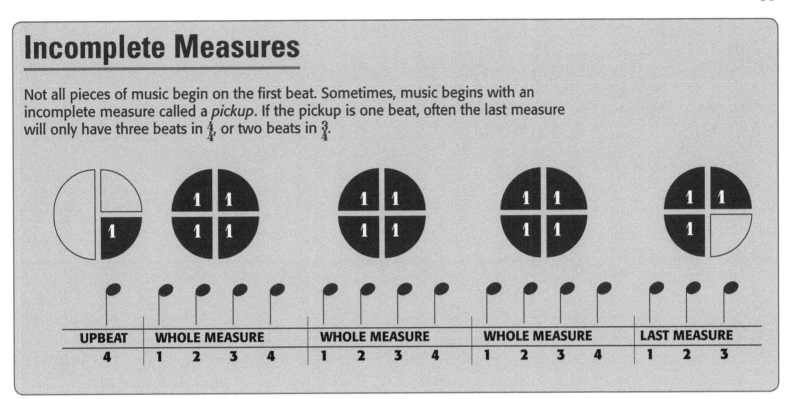

Here is another song for you to sing while you play the accompaniment.

A-TISKET, A-TASKET

Track 40
Melody and Chords

Track 41
Chords Only

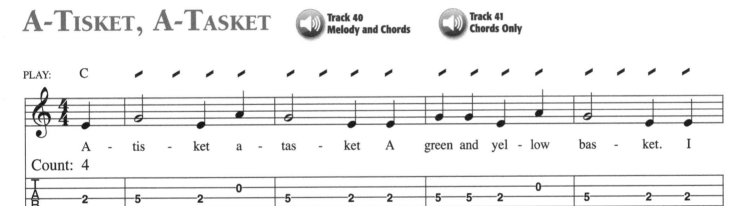

Ties

This curved line is called a *tie*. It connects two or more notes and ties them together. Play or sing the note once and hold it for the value of both (or more) tied notes. In TAB, a tied note is shown as a number in parentheses; do not pick that note again.

TOM DOOLEY

Track 42
Melody and Chords

Track 43
Chords Only

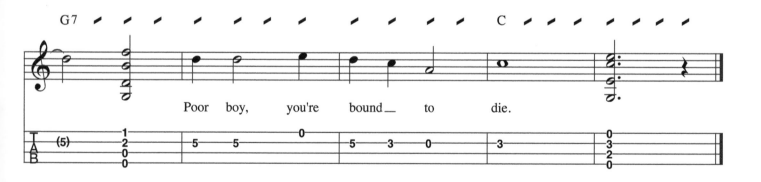

Eighth Notes

Eighth notes are black notes that have a flag added to the stem: ♪ or ♭ .
Two or more eighth notes are written with a *beam*: ♫ or ⊔ .

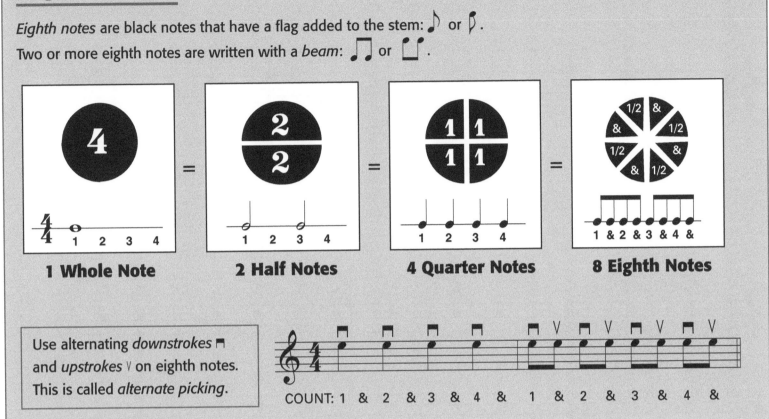

| 1 Whole Note | 2 Half Notes | 4 Quarter Notes | 8 Eighth Notes |

Use alternating *downstrokes* ⊓ and *upstrokes* ∨ on eighth notes. This is called *alternate picking*.

COUNT: 1 & 2 & 3 & 4 & 1 & 2 & 3 & 4 &

JAMMIN' WITH EIGHTH NOTES

Track 44
Melody and Chords

Track 45
Chords Only

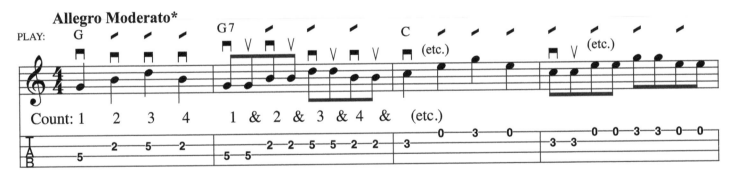

Allegro Moderato*

Count: 1   2   3   4   1 & 2 & 3 & 4 &   (etc.)

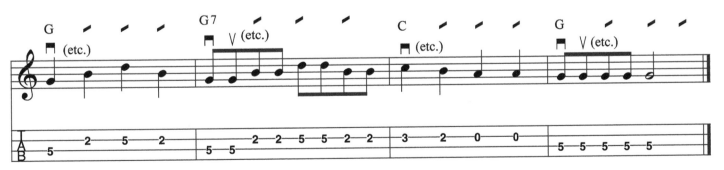

Allegro moderato means moderately fast.

Go Tell Aunt Rhody

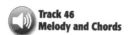
Track 46
Melody and Chords

Track 47
Chords Only

Moderato

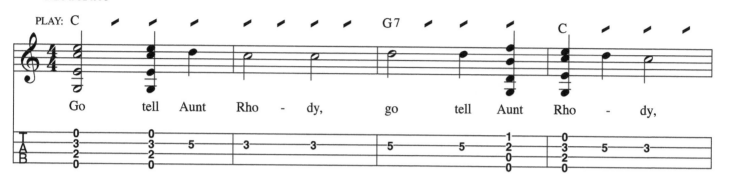

Go tell Aunt Rho - dy, go tell Aunt Rho - dy,

go tell Aunt Rho - dy that the old gray goose is dead._____ The

one we've been sav - ing, the one we've been sav - ing, the

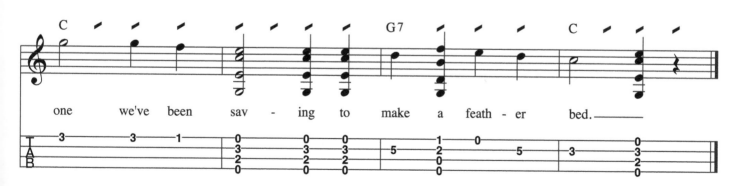

one we've been sav - ing to make a feath - er bed._____

Dotted Quarter Notes

A DOT INCREASES THE LENGTH
OF A NOTE BY ONE HALF.

Preparatory Drill

The only difference in the
following two measures and
those directly above them is the
way they are written.
They should sound the SAME.

In "Auld Lang Syne," play the melody and have your teacher or friend play the accompaniment.
This song features many dotted quarter note rhythms.

AULD LANG SYNE Track 48

CLEMENTINE

  **Track 49** Melody and Chords   **Track 50** Chords Only

Moderato

Additional Verses

Light she was and like a fairy,
And her shoes were number nine,

Herring boxes, without topses,
Sandals were for Clementine.

Oh my darlin', oh my darlin',
Oh my darlin', Clementine!

Thou art lost and gone forever
Dreadful sorry, Clementine.

Drove she ducklings to the water,
Ev'ry morning just at nine,

Hit her foot against a splinter,
Fell into the foaming brine.

Oh my darlin', oh my darlin',
Oh my darlin', Clementine!

Thou art lost and gone forever
Dreadful sorry, Clementine.

Ruby lips above the water,
Blowing bubbles, soft and fine,

But, alas, I was no swimmer,
So I lost my Clementine.

Oh my darlin', oh my darlin',
Oh my darlin', Clementine!

Thou art lost and gone forever
Dreadful sorry, Clementine.

Sharps ♯, Flats ♭, and Naturals ♮

The distance from one fret to the next fret, up or down, is a *half step.* Two half steps make a *whole step.*

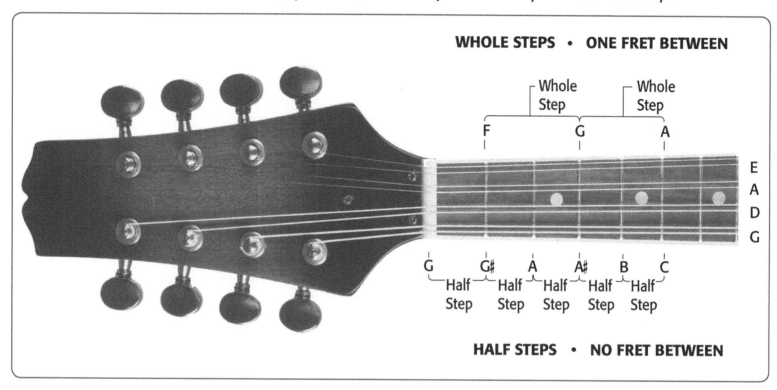

SHARPS ♯ **raise** the note a half step. Play the next fret higher.

FLATS ♭ **lower** the note a half step. If the note is fingered, play the next fret lower.
If the note is open, play the 6th fret of the next lower string.

NATURALS ♮ **cancel** a previous sharp or flat.

When added within a measure, sharps, flats, and naturals are called *accidentals.*
A bar line cancels a previous accidental in the measures that follow.

A note that is sharp or flat continues to be flat or sharp in the same measure unless it is cancelled by a natural. Flats and sharps only last until the end of the measure.

The chromatic scale includes all the notes you know on all four strings, including the sharps (going up) and flats (going down). There is a new note, high B, which is played on the 7th fret of the first string. Be sure to use the fingerings marked above the music.

THE CHROMATIC SCALE Track 51

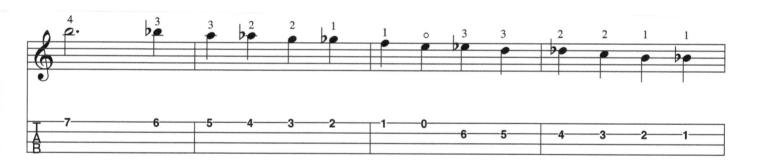

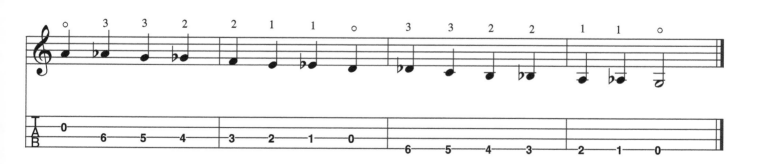

44

This song uses a few of the chromatic notes you just learned. Remember, a sharp or flat note is in effect for the entire measure unless it is cancelled by a natural.

MY MELANCHOLY BABY Track 52

G. Norton and
E. Burnett

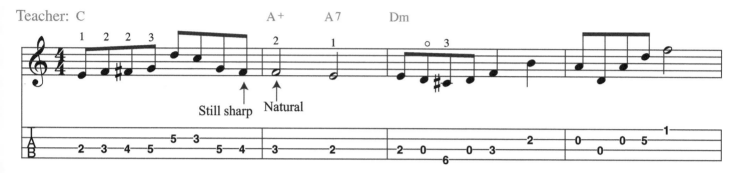

Still sharp Natural

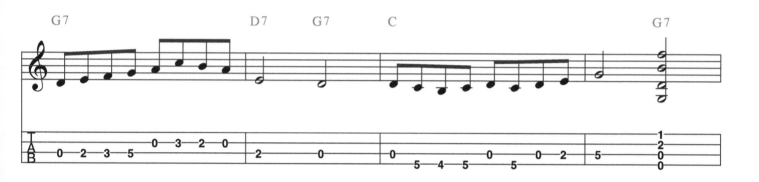

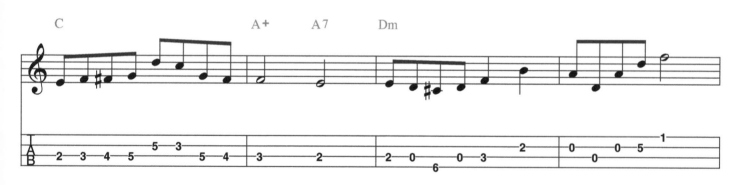

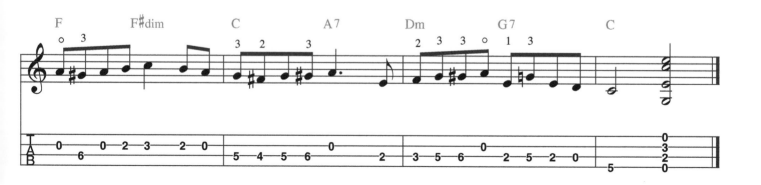

The D Chord

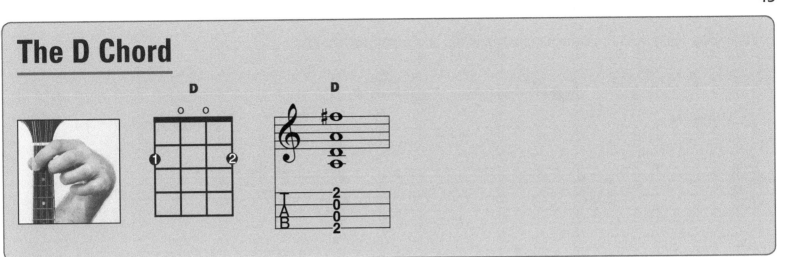

Track 53

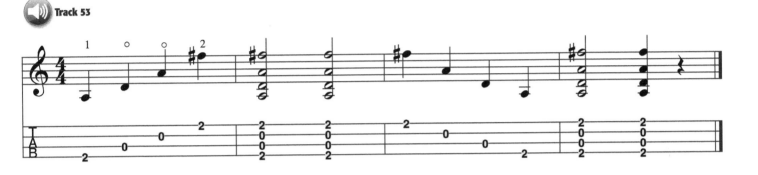

The D7 Chord

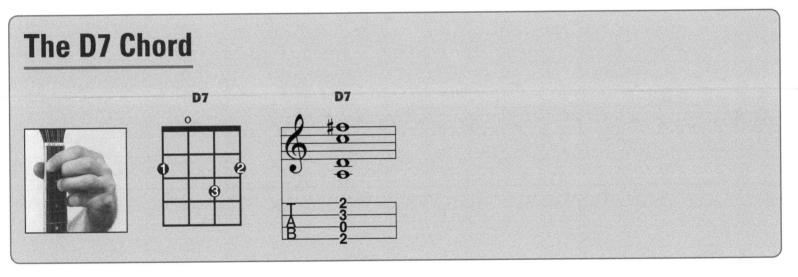

Track 54

For this song, learn both the written melody and the accompanying chords.

BACH MINUET

Track 55
Melody and Chords

Track 56
Chords Only

Moderato

Attributed to J. S. Bach

Play "Buffalo Gals" in two ways: first as a musically complete mandolin solo, then as accompaniment while you sing. Strum chords once on each beat. Note that in the written arrangement, the chords do not use all four strings. These are called *broken chords* and they make the arrangement more interesting. When the bass note comes before the chord, hold all the fingers down of the chord so all the strings sound strong.

BUFFALO GALS

Track 57 Melody and Chords   **Track 58** Chords Only

Dynamics

Signs showing how soft or loud to play are called *dynamics*.

The most common dynamics are shown here. The words in parentheses are the Italian names for each dynamic.

 (piano) **soft**    (mezzo-forte) **moderately loud**   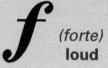 (forte) **loud**   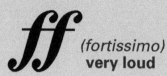 (fortissimo) **very loud**

ECHO WALTZ

Track 59 Melody and Chords   Track 60 Chords Only

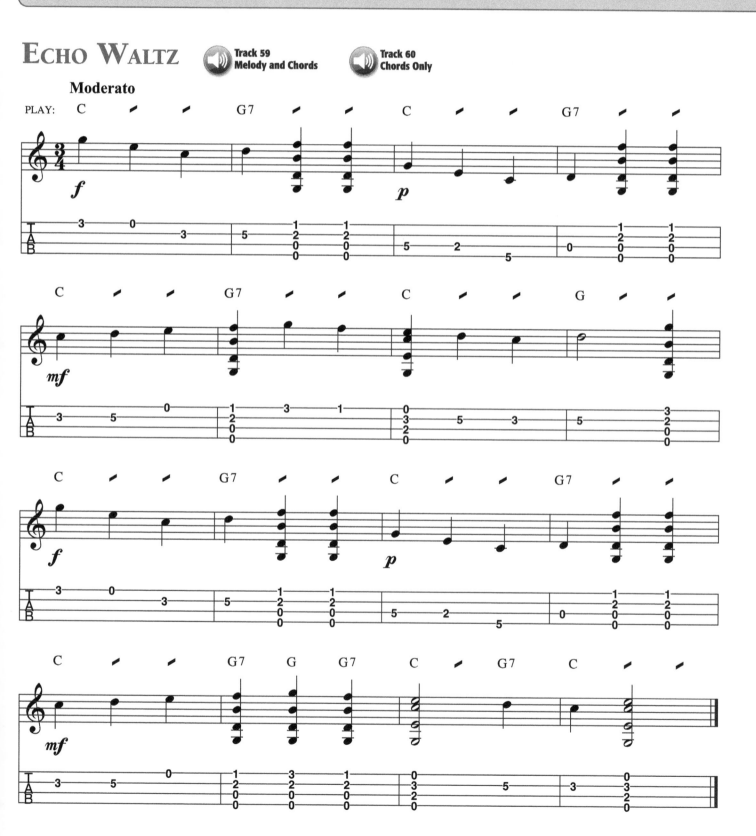

Eighth Rests

This is an *eighth rest*.
It means to rest for the value of an eighth note.

Single eighth notes are often used with eighth rests:

COUNT: 1 &

Clap or tap the following rhythm:

COUNT: 1 & 2 & 3 & 4 &

EIGHTH REST EXERCISE NO. 1 Track 61

When playing a fingered note, cut off the sound by releasing the pressure of the finger on the string. When playing an open note, the sound is cut off by touching the string with either a left-hand finger or the heel of your right hand.

COUNT: 1 & 2 & 3 & 4 & etc.

EIGHTH REST EXERCISE NO. 2 Track 62

Eighth rests may also appear on downbeats. This creates no problem if the student marks the downbeat by tapping the foot or mentally counting.

COUNT: 1 & 2 & 3 & 4 & 1 & 2 & 3 & 4 & 1 & 2 & 3 & 4 & 1 & 2 & 3 & 4 &

BILL BAILEY  Track 63

Moderate Ragtime Tempo

H. Cannon

Teacher: G

Count: 1 & 2 & 1 & 2 & etc.

The Drone

Some of the most popular music for the mandolin was originally written for fiddle (violin).
Fiddles and mandolins are tuned to the same notes so these two instruments make a great
combination in a bluegrass band. One of the most distinct sounds a fiddle makes happens
when the fiddle player plays a melody along with an adjacent open string. The sound the
open string makes against the melody is called a *drone*. It sounds very much like the sound a
bagpipe makes. This arrangement of "Amazing Grace" uses drones on the G and D strings.

AMAZING GRACE Track 64

English Hymn

Sixteenth Notes

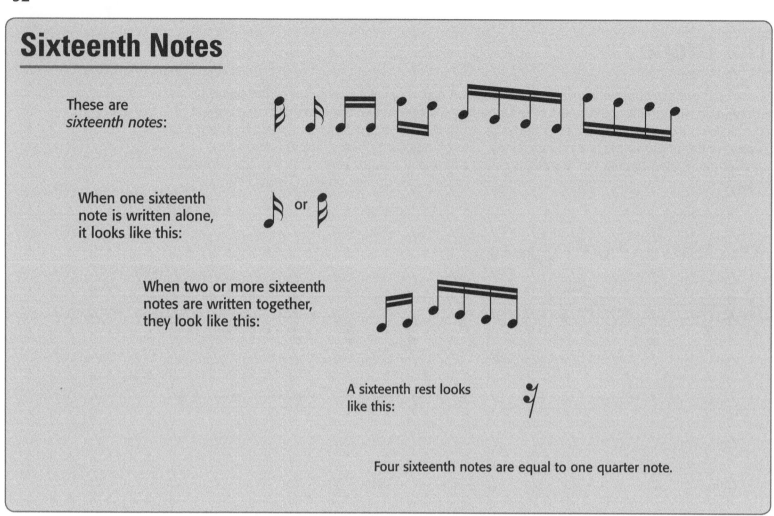

These are *sixteenth notes*:

When one sixteenth note is written alone, it looks like this:

When two or more sixteenth notes are written together, they look like this:

A sixteenth rest looks like this:

Four sixteenth notes are equal to one quarter note.

Two sixteenth notes are played in the time of one eighth note. Like eighth notes, use alternate picking (up-down-up-down) when playing sixteenths. Make sure to play each note evenly and count 1-e-&-a, 2-e-&-a, etc.

SIXTEENTH NOTE EXERCISE 🔊 Track 65

Moderato

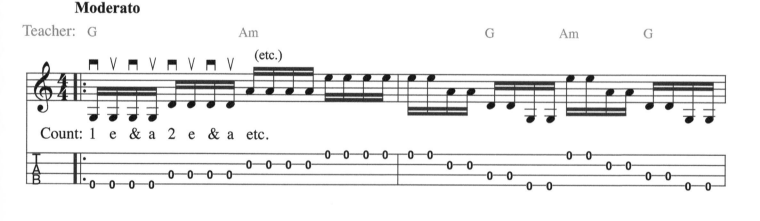

This version of "Drunken Sailor" uses both sixteenth and drone notes.

DRUNKEN SAILOR Track 66

Teacher: Am

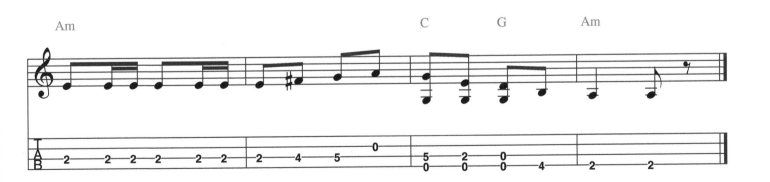

The Tremolo

When playing notes and chords on the mandolin, the sound tends to die off quickly. If the music you are playing has a whole note tied to a half note, you probably won't be able to hear the half note at all. One of the most characteristic sounds on the mandolin solves this problem and it is called the *tremolo*. Tremolo is rapid picking of a note that allows that note to be heard for as long as you play it.

Tremolo is notated by three short diagonal lines ⫽ either directly above or below a note.

TREMOLO EXERCISE NO. 1   🔊 Track 67

Stop tremolo here

When you see a tremolo, rapidly pick the note with an alternate picking pattern (up-down, up-down, etc.) with fast, even strokes. It should almost sound like a single sustained note.

Remember, you are actually playing two strings at once since each note in the music is actually a course of two strings. The tremolo is a rapid playing of both of those strings. When you play a tremolo that is tied to a note that isn't a tremolo, stop the tremolo and let the second note ring its normal length.

It is important that you count to make sure you are playing the correct length of a note, but you do not need to count how many times you pick the tremolo. Let your picking hand pick the tremolo quickly and evenly, but make sure you don't play the note longer or shorter than the standard note value.

In the next example, start off very slowly and make sure to keep the notes even. When you play the tremolo, you aren't playing sixteenth notes like the previous measure; you should be playing a bit faster than sixteenths, but the length of the whole note should still equal four full beats—no more, no less. Gradually increase the speed of the exercise until you are playing the tremolo quickly and evenly.

TREMOLO EXERCISE NO. 2   🔊 Track 68

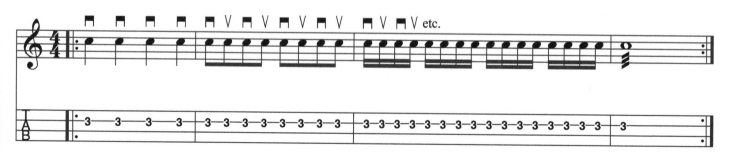

SHENANDOAH

Track 69

Traditional American Folk Song

Teacher:

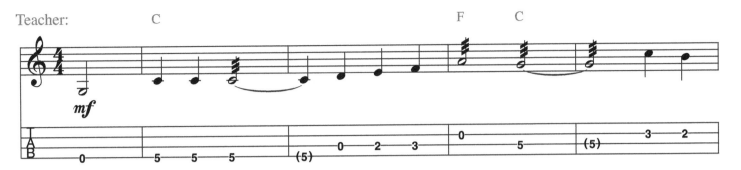

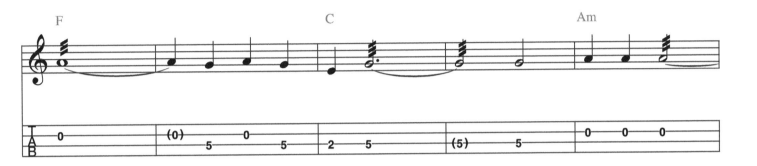

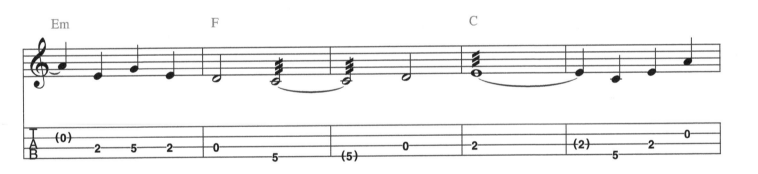

The Major Scale

A *scale* is a succession of notes in alphabetical order. All *major scales* are built using the same sequence of eight steps:
**whole step, whole step, half step,
whole step, whole step, whole step, half step.**

The highest note of the scale, having the same letter name as the first note, is called the *octave* note.

C Major Scale

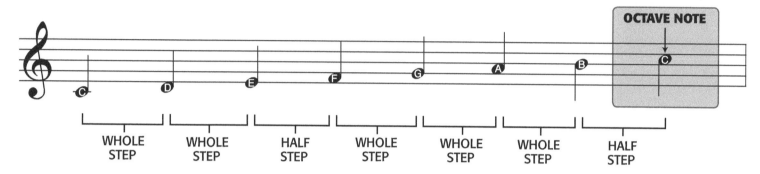

It is easier to visualize whole steps and half steps on a piano keyboard. Notice there are whole steps between every natural note except E–F and B–C.

Whole steps: One key between

Half steps: No key between

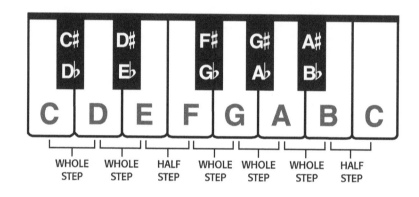

A major scale may be built starting on any note, whether natural, sharp, or flat.
Using the pattern you just learned, write a major scale starting on G.

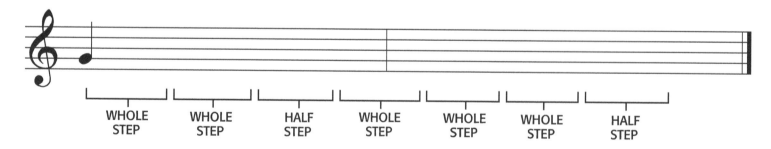

Using the pattern, write a major scale starting on F.

Check: Are the notes in alphabetical order?

Key Signatures

The Key of C Major

A piece based on the C Major scale is in the *key of C Major*.

The Key of G Major

A piece based on the G Major scale is in the *key of G Major*. Since F is sharp in the G Major scale, every F will be sharp in the key of G Major. Instead of making all the F's sharp in the piece, the sharp is indicated at the beginning of the music in the *key signature*. Sharps or flats shown in the key signature are effective throughout the piece.

Key Signature
One Sharp (F♯)

The Key of F Major

A piece based on the F Major scale is in the *key of F Major*. Since B is flat in the F Major scale, every B will be flat in the key of F Major.

Key Signature
One Flat (B♭)

Accidentals Review

If sharps, flats, or naturals not shown in the key signature occur in the piece, they are called *accidentals*. Accidentals are effective only for the measures in which they appear.

The three scales shown above should be practiced everyday. Students who do this will have little difficulty playing selections written in C Major, G Major, and F Major.

This song is in the key of G, and the key signature has one sharp. Every note F is played F-sharp.

In order to keep the drone in the 12th full measure, the note A is played on the 3rd string and not the open second string. To do this, shift your hand up the neck for one beat and play the A with your 4th finger on the 7th fret. Practice moving your 4th finger from the A back to the G a few times to play it smooth and in steady time.

SHE'LL BE COMIN' 'ROUND THE MOUNTAIN

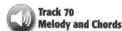

Additional Verses

She'll be drivin' six white horses
when she comes, etc.

Oh we'll all come out to meet her
when she comes, etc.

She'll be wearing pink pajamas
when she comes, etc.

We will kill the old red rooster when
she comes, etc.

We'll all be shoutin' "Halleluja"
when she comes, etc.

She'll be comin' down a road that's
five miles long, etc.

Downstrokes and Upstrokes

You can make your accompaniment of waltz songs in $\frac{3}{4}$, like "The Streets of Laredo," more interesting by replacing the second beat of the measure with a downstroke followed by an upstroke. Remember, the symbol for downstroke is ⊓; an upstroke uses the symbol V. Together, the down and upstroke are played in the same time as a regular strum.

Try the following exercise to work just on the new rhythm first.

Track 72

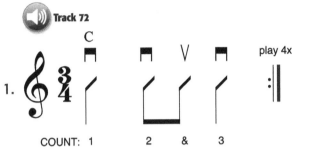

Now practice changing from C to G7.

Track 73

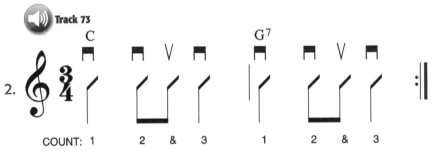

Now practice changing back and forth from C to G7 and back. When you can do it smoothly, use this strum with the chords to accompany yourself singing "The Streets of Laredo."

Track 74

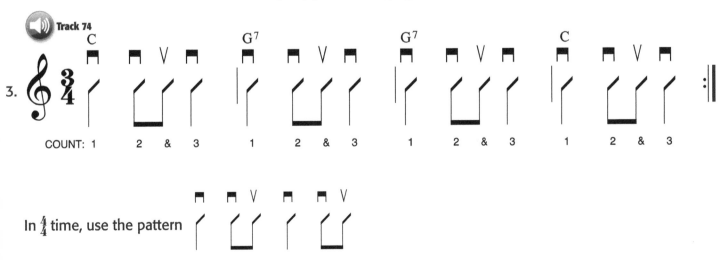

In $\frac{4}{4}$ time, use the pattern

This song is in the key of C so there are no sharps or flats. It uses a G drone through most of the song. Play the arrangement first and get used to the melody. Then play the chords with the downstrokes and upstrokes you learned on page 59, and sing along.

THE STREETS OF LAREDO

Track 75
Melody and Chords

Track 76
Chords Only

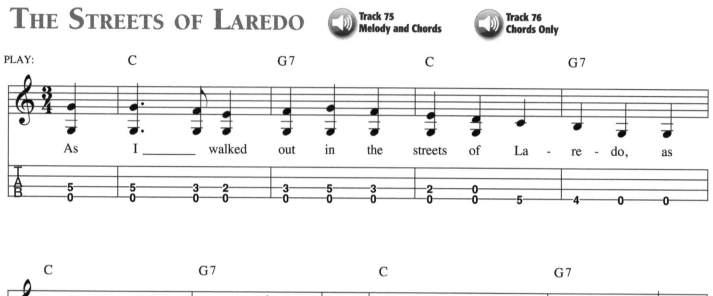

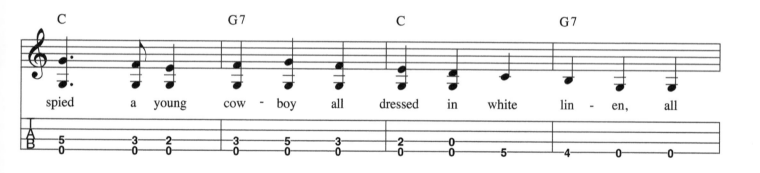

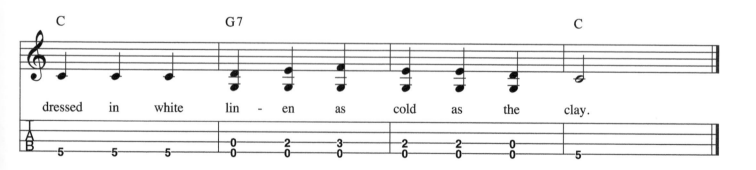

$\frac{6}{8}$ Time

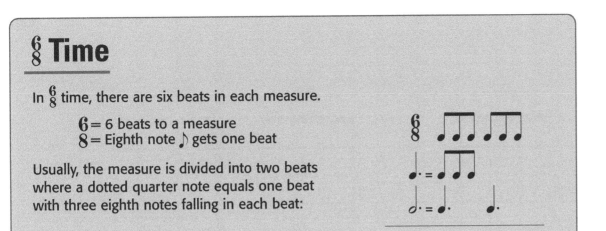

In $\frac{6}{8}$ time, there are six beats in each measure.

$\mathbf{6}$ = 6 beats to a measure
$\mathbf{8}$ = Eighth note $\flat$ gets one beat

Usually, the measure is divided into two beats where a dotted quarter note equals one beat with three eighth notes falling in each beat:

This tune is in the key of G so every F is sharp.

THE IRISH WASHERWOMAN

Track 77 Melody and Chords

Track 78 Chords Only

* Both of these picking patterns work for $\frac{6}{8}$ time. Pick the one more comfortable for you.

The A7 Chord

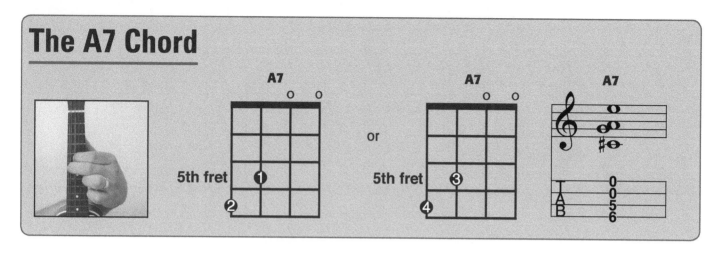

This is one of the most popular songs of all time. First learn the melody, and then play the chords and sing. Feel free to add more tremolos to make your playing more expressive.

Over the Rainbow

Track 79
Melody and Chords

Track 80
Chords Only

Words by E. Y. Harburg
Music by Harold Arlen

Moderato

Some - where o - ver the rain - bow way up high,

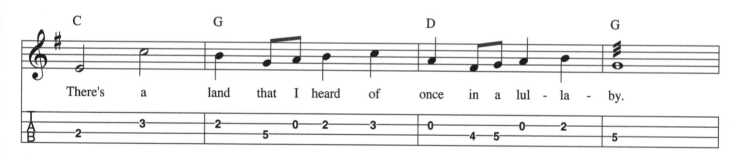

There's a land that I heard of once in a lul - la - by.

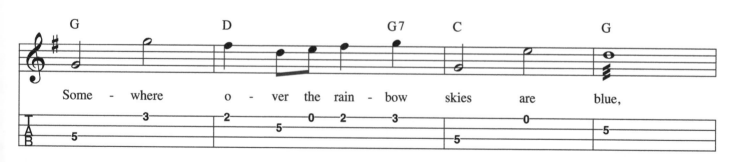

Some - where o - ver the rain - bow skies are blue,

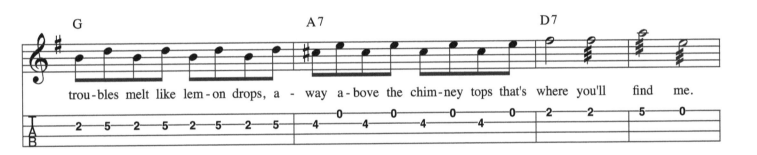

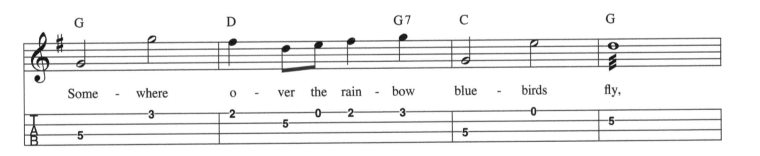

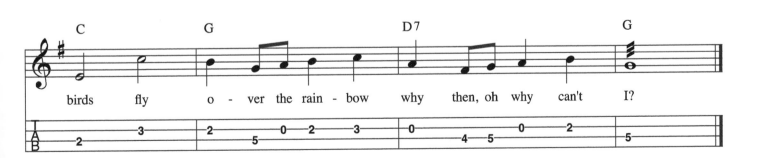

CERTIFICATE OF PROMOTION

ALFRED'S BASIC MANDOLIN METHOD

This certifies that

has mastered

Alfred's Basic Mandolin Method 1

and is promoted to

Alfred's Basic Mandolin Method 2

Teacher _____

Date _____